The King Salmon Cookbook

Gain creativity, tastefulness and a perfect weight balance with these delicious, quick and easy recipes, thought to improve your muscles and boost your mental energy. Expand your beginner skills and learn step by step how to use this amazing fish.

Ernest Pescara

Table of Contents

Welcome, dear!

This is my offer to your cooking style.

This cookbook is the realization of my research on how to eat tasty and healthy food at the meantime.
My purpose is to increase your energies and to let you live a lighter life, without the junk of the globalised kitchen.

In here, you'll find my knowledge on how to create delicious dishes with salmon.

Jump into a worldwide discovery of good food and natural-feed animals, with many recipes for a varied diet.

Nevertheless, you'll learn new techniques, discover tastes of all around the world and improve your skills.
Let yourself be inspired by the worldwide traditions, twisted by a proper chef.

Each of these dishes is thought to:

1 – Let you understand how to work with Salmon
This majestic animal is offered in various presentations of different cultures, to show you how the same ingredient can change from dish to dish.

2 – Balance your weight with different cooking methods
As soon as you learn different ways to cook your fish, you'll discover an entire world of new ideas.
Salmon will never bore you again!

3 – Amaze your friends starting from the smell
Once your friends will come to dinner, they will be in love with your food even before to see your creation.

The King Salmon Cookbook

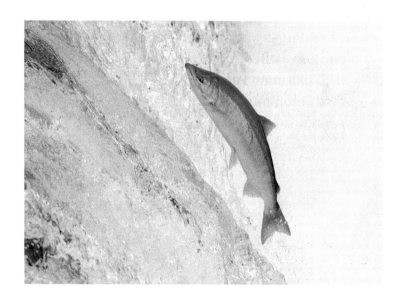

Honey-Glazed Salmon Steaks

Serves 2 pax

Ingredients

- 1 tbsp runny honey
- 1 garlic clove, peeled and crushed
- Salt and freshly ground black pepper
- 1 cup Olive oil
- 1 tbsp balsamic vinegar
- 1 tbsp Dijon mustard
- 2 salmon steaks

Procedure

1. Mix together the vinegar, mustard, honey, garlic and seasoning in a bowl.
2. Brush over both sides of the salmon and leave in the fridge for about an hour.
3. Heat a ridged frying pan to a very high heat, then rub it with a little oil.
4. Sear the steaks for about 3 minutes on each side, turning only once. The fish is cooked if it flakes easily when lightly prised with a fork.
5. The cooking time may vary depending on the thickness of the salmon steaks and how you like them cooked.
6. Remove from the grill, brush with any remaining glaze.
7. Serve.

Salmon and Spinaches Salad

Ingredients

- 1 cup Dried cranberries
- 1 cup Canola oil
- 1 tbsp Balsamic vinaigrette
- 2 Avocado
- 1 Salmon fillet
- 1 oz Spinach
- 1 cup Sunflower kernels
- 1 cup Walnuts
- Salt and Pepper

Procedure

1. Place a large skillet and oil on a moderate fire and place in the salmon fillets. Sprinkle with pepper and salt.
2. Cook it until the fish flakes easily.
3. Place your spinach in a bowl and pour in the vinaigrette.
4. Toss to evenly coat and serve on plates.
5. Place the salmon on the spinach and top with the remaining ingredients.

Salmon in 5 Spices

Serves 2 pax

Ingredients

- 2 (6-ounce) salmon fillets, washed and patted dry
- 2 teaspoons lime juice
- 1/2teaspoon Chinese 5-spice powder
- 1 tablespoon unsalted butter
- 1 cup Vegetable oil

Procedure

1. Using paper towels, wipe a thin coat of vegetable oil over a broiler pan.

2. Preheat your broiler on high, with the rack set on the upper third of the oven.

3. Melt the butter using low heat in a small deep cooking pan. Mix in the 5-spice powder and lime juice; keep warm.

4. Put the salmon on the broiler pan, skin side up. Broil for two to 4 minutes or until the skin is crunchy.

5. Turn the salmon over and broil two minutes more or until done to your preference.

6. Move the salmon to 2 plates and spoon the butter sauce over the top.

Roasted Salmon Filets

Serves 4 pax

Ingredients

- 1 Tbsp Lime juice
- 1 Tbsp Freshly grated ginger
- 1 Tbsp Serrano chile pepper
- 1 Tbsp Olive oil
- 4x 4 oz Salmon filets
- 1 Tbsp Brown sugar blend
- 2 Tbsp Soy sauce

Procedure

1. Set the oven temperature at 375° Fahrenheit.

2. Stir together all ingredients except the salmon, then pour it over the salmon in a dish small enough so the marinade will cover each side of the fish.

3. Refrigerate to marinate for 30 minutes. Preheat the grill.

4. Grill the salmon for four to six minutes per side. Discard the remaining marinade.

5. If you prefer to bake this, prepare a baking dish with cooking oil spray.

6. Place it in the dish and bake for eight to ten minutes per side until just opaque.

Whole-Wheat Salmon Spaghetti

Ingredients

- 1 (15-ounce) can cannellini beans, rinsed
- 1 onion, chopped fine
- 1 pound whole-wheat spaghetti
- 2 pounds curly-leaf spinach, stemmed and cut into 1-inch pieces
- 5 ounces Parmesan cheese, grated (1 cup), plus extra for serving
- 3 tablespoons extra-virgin olive oil, plus extra for serving
- 1 Salmon fillet
- 1/2teaspoon red pepper flakes
- 3/4 cup pitted kalamata olives, chopped coarse
- 3/4 cup vegetable broth
- 1 (14.5-ounce) can diced tomatoes, drained
- 8 garlic cloves, peeled (5 sliced thin along the length, 3 minced)
- Salt and pepper

Procedure

1. Cook oil and sliced garlic in 12-inch straight-sided sauté pan on moderate heat, stirring frequently, until garlic turns golden but not brown, approximately three minutes. Use a slotted spoon to move garlic to plate coated using paper towels and season lightly with salt; set aside.

2. Put in onion to oil left in pan and cook on moderate heat till they become tender and lightly browned, 5 to 7 minutes. Mix in minced garlic, pepper flakes, salmon and cook until aromatic, approximately half a minute.

3. Put in half of spinach and cook, tossing occasionally, until starting to wilt, approximately two minutes. Put in remaining spinach, broth, tomatoes, and 3/4 teaspoon salt and bring to simmer.

4. Decrease heat to medium, cover (pan will be very full), and cook, tossing occasionally, until spinach is completely wilted, about 10 minutes (mixture will be somewhat soupy). Remove from the heat, mix in beans and olives.

5. In the meantime, bring 4 quarts water to boil in large pot. Put in pasta and 1 tablespoon salt and cook, stirring frequently, until just shy of al dente. Reserve 1/2cup cooking water, then drain pasta and return it to pot.

6. Put in greens mixture and cook on moderate heat, tossing to combine, until pasta absorbs most of liquid, approximately two minutes.

7. Remove from the heat, mix in Parmesan. Sprinkle with salt and pepper to taste and regulate consistency with reserved cooking water as required.

8. Serve, sprinkling individual portions with garlic chips and extra Parmesan and drizzling with extra oil.

Zucchini Farfalle and Salmon

Serves 6 pax

Ingredients

- 2 garlic cloves, minced
- 1 Salmon fillet
- 1/4 cup chopped fresh mint
- 1/2cup pitted kalamata olives, quartered
- 18 pounds farfalle
- 1 red onion, chopped fine
- 1 teaspoon grated lemon zest plus 1 tablespoon juice
- 12 ounces grape tomatoes, halved
- 3 pounds zucchini and/or summer squash, halved along the length and sliced 1/2inch thick
- 3 teaspoons red wine vinegar
- 12 ounces feta cheese, crumbled
- 4 tablespoons extra-virgin olive oil
- Kosher salt and pepper

Procedure

1. Toss squash with 1 tablespoon salt and allow to drain using a colander for 30 minutes. Pat squash dry using paper towels and carefully wipe away any residual salt.

2. Heat 1 tablespoon oil in 12-inch non-stick frying pan on high heat until just smoking. Put in half of squash and salmon and cook, stirring intermittently, until golden brown and mildly charred, 5 to 7 minutes, reducing heat if frying pan begins to scorch; move to large plate.

3. Repeat with 1 tablespoon oil and remaining squash; move to plate.

4. Heat 1 tablespoon oil in now-empty frying pan on moderate heat until it starts to shimmer. Put in onion and cook till they become tender and lightly browned, 5 to 7 minutes.

5. Mix in garlic, lemon zest, and 1/2teaspoon pepper and cook until aromatic, approximately half a minute. Mix in squash and cook until heated through, approximately half a minute.

6. In the meantime, bring 4 quarts water to boil in large pot. Put in pasta and 1 tablespoon salt and cook, stirring frequently, until al dente.

7. Reserve 1/2cup cooking water, then drain pasta and return it to pot. Put in squash mixture, tomatoes, olives, mint, vinegar, lemon juice, and remaining 2 tablespoons oil and toss to combine.

8. Sprinkle with salt and pepper to taste and serve.

Grilled Salmon, Chilean Sauce

Ingredients

- 1 (13 by 9 inch) disposable aluminum roasting pan
- 1 teaspoon grated lime zest
- 6 tablespoons juice (3 limes)
- 2 garlic cloves, minced
- 3 tablespoons chopped fresh cilantro
- 4 tablespoons vegetable oil
- 2 tablespoons unsalted butter
- 1/2teaspoon ground cumin
- 1 (10 ounce) skin on salmon steaks, 2 inches thick
- Salt and pepper

Procedure

1. Pat salmon steaks dry using paper towels. Working with 1 steak at a time, cautiously trim 11/2inches of skin from 1 tail.

2. Firmly wrap other tail around skinned portion and tie steaks using a kitchen twine. Season salmon with salt and pepper and brush both sides with oil. Mix lime zest and juice, butter, garlic, cumin, and 1/8 teaspoon salt in disposable pan.

3. On a GAS GRILL: Set all burners to high, cover, and heat grill until hot, approximately fifteen minutes. Leave primary burner on high and turn off other burner(s).

4. Clean cooking grate, then constantly brush grate with well oiled paper towels until black and shiny, five to ten times.

5. Put salmon on hotter part of grill. Cook until browned on both sides, two to three minutes per side.

6. In the meantime, set disposable pan on cooler part of grill and cook until butter has melted, approximately 2 minutes.

7. Move salmon to pan and gently turn to coat. Cook salmon (covered if using gas) until center is still translucent when checked with tip of paring knife and records 125 degrees (for medium rare), six to fourteen minutes, turning salmon and rotating pan midway through grilling.

8. Move salmon to platter; remove twine. Whisk cilantro into sauce left in pan.

9. Sprinkle sauce over salmon before you serve.

Guaca Salsa for Salmon

Serves 6 pax

Ingredients

- 1/4 teaspoon salt
- 1/8 teaspoon fresh ground black pepper
- 1/2 avocado, pitted and diced
- 1/4 cup fresh cilantro, chopped
- 1 large tomato, diced
- 1/4 cup red onion, diced
- 1/2 jalapeno pepper, minced
- 5 tablespoons fresh squeezed lime juice
- 1 pinch cayenne pepper

Procedure

1. Combine tomato, onion, minced jalapeno, lime juice, salt and pepper in bowl.
2. Add avocado, cilantro and cayenne.
3. Stir until well mixed.
4. Refrigerate.

Salmon Steaks, Chard and Coconut Sauce

Ingredients

- 1 (2 inches) fresh ginger piece
- 4 salmon steaks or fillets
- Sea salt and freshly ground black pepper
- A handful of Chard, when held by the stalks
- A glug of olive oil
- 1 large onion, peeled and thinly sliced
- 4 tomatoes, deseeded and chopped
- 1 tsp sugar
- 1/2 mug coconut milk
- 1/2 mug water
- Juice of 1 lime
- 1 handful of chopped fresh coriander

Procedure

1. Slice the ginger and cut into slivers (it's not necessary to peel the ginger – just cut off any tough bits). Season the salmon with salt and pepper and set aside.

2. Strip the chard leaves from the stalks and roughly chop the leaves. Dice the stalks into small pieces.

3. Heat the oil in a wide, deep frying pan over a medium heat. Add the onion, ginger and chard stems and cook, stirring occasionally, for about 5 minutes.

4. Add the chopped tomatoes and the sugar and continue to cook for another 4–5 minutes. Add the coconut milk and water and season well with salt and pepper. Stir, bring to the boil, then simmer over a low heat for a further 15 minutes.

5. Stir in the chard leaves, squeeze the lime over them and arrange the salmon pieces in a single layer over the top of the sauce. Spoon some of the liquid over the fish.

6. Cover with a tight-fitting lid, return to a medium heat, and simmer for about 10 minutes, or until the fish is just cooked through.

7. To serve, lift the fish and chard sauce onto a hot serving dish.

8. Spoon the remaining liquid over the top of the fish, garnish with coriander and serve immediately with rice.

Grilled Medallions of Salmon

Serves 6 pax

Ingredients

- 1 large salmon fillet
- 3 tbsp extra-virgin olive oil

Procedure

1. Preheat grill.
2. Brush salmon liberally with oil. Grill salmon, brushing with oil as needed. When salmon is done, cut into medallions.
3. Garnish linguini pasta with salmon medallions.
4. Serve immediately.

Salmon Tartare and Avocado

Ingredients

- 4 ounces smoked Alaskan salmon sliced thin
- 1 garlic clove, chopped very fine
- 1/4 teaspoon fresh ground black pepper
- 1 pinch cayenne pepper
- 3 shallots, chopped very fine
- 1 tablespoon fresh squeezed lemon juice
- 1/2teaspoon salt
- 14 ounces fresh Alaskan salmon fillet
- 4 drops Worcestershire sauce

Procedure

1. Remove skin from salmon. Cut fillet and smoked salmon slices into 1/4" strips.
2. Combine salmon in bowl with all other ingredients. Mix until thoroughly combined.
3. Line four 3" ramekins with plastic wrap, let edges project.
4. Divide tartare mix evenly amongst ramekins. Press tops lightly until smooth.
5. Turn ramekins out onto serving plates. Remove plastic wrap.
6. Serve.

Grilled Salmon, Pesto and Watercress

Serves 4 pax

Ingredients

- 1/4 cup chopped peeled fresh ginger
- 1/4 teaspoon cayenne pepper
- 7 tablespoons vegetable oil
- Salt and freshly ground black pepper to taste
- 1 cup chopped fresh cilantro
- ½ cup chopped green onions
- 1/3 cup salted roasted macadamia nuts
- 4 x 6-ounce pieces salmon fillet
- 1 large garlic clove, minced
- 3 tablespoons olive oil
- 2 bunches of watercress, coarse stems discarded and the watercress rinsed but not spun dry

Procedure

1. Combine first 5 ingredients in food processor. Blend until nuts are finely chopped. Add 6 tablespoons oil and process until well blended. Season to taste with salt and pepper.
2. Prepare grill.
3. Brush salmon with remaining 1 tablespoon vegetable oil and sprinkle with salt and pepper to taste. Grill salmon on an oiled rack set 5 to 6 inches over glowing coals until just cooked through, about 5 minutes on each side.
4. Meanwhile, in a large heavy skillet sauté the garlic in the olive oil over moderately high heat for 30 seconds, or until it is fragrant.
5. Add the watercress and stir the mixture until it is combined well. Sauté the watercress, covered, for 2 to 3 minutes, or until it is just wilted, and Season to taste with salt and pepper.
6. To serve, put sautéed watercress in the center of 4 plates. Top with the salmon and spoon pesto around. Serve basmati rice alongside.
7. Serve with basmati rice.

Phyllo Salmon, Shiitake and Champagne

Serves 6 pax

Ingredients

- 1/2teaspoon freshly ground black pepper
- 3 garlic cloves, minced
- 1 lemon, thinly sliced
- 3 pounds salmon fillet
- 1/4 cup chopped scallions
- 15 x 6 x 3/8-inch cedar grilling plank
- ½ cup rice vinegar
- ½ cup low-sodium soy sauce
- 4 tablespoons honey
- 1 teaspoon ground ginger
- 1 tablespoon sesame seeds, toasted

Procedure

1. Immerse and soak the plank in water 1 hour; drain.
2. To prepare grill for indirect grilling, heat one side of the grill to high heat.
3. Combine vinegar and the next 6 ingredients (vinegar through lemon) in a large zip-top plastic bag; seal.
4. Shake to combine. Add fish; seal. Marinate in refrigerator 30 minutes, turning once.
5. Place plank on grill rack over high heat; grill 5 minutes or until lightly charred. Carefully turn plank over; move to cool side of grill.
6. Remove fish from marinade; discard marinade. Place fish, skin side down, on charred side of plank.
7. Cover and grill 15 minutes or until fish flakes easily when tested with a fork.
8. To serve, place on bed of Pickled Ginger and Watercress Salad (recipe follows) on 6 plates.
9. Top with portions of salmon and sprinkle with scallions and sesame seeds.

Pickled Ginger and Watercress Salad

Ingredients

- 1 tablespoon fresh lime juice or rice wine vinegar
- 1 tablespoon canola oil
- 1 teaspoon honey
- 1 clove garlic, crushed
- 1/8 teaspoon kosher salt
- 1 tablespoon liquid from a jar of picked ginger
- Freshly ground black pepper to taste
- 6 cups stemmed, washed and dried watercress
- 4 scallions, chopped
- 1/3 cup drained pickled ginger

Procedure

1. With the side of a chef's knife, mash garlic with salt.
2. Place in a small bowl or a jar with a tightfitting lid.
3. Add ginger liquid, lime juice (or vinegar), oil, honey and pepper; whisk or shake until blended.
4. Place watercress, scallions and pickled ginger in a large bowl.
5. Just before serving, toss with dressing.

Seafood Linguini and Salmon

Ingredients

- 8 ounces clams (cooked, drained and chopped)
- 1 pound fresh scallops (raw)
- 1 cup lobster stock
- 18 pounds fresh linguine
- 1 ounce butter
- 8 ounces mussel meat
- 1 cup heavy cream

Procedure

1. Cook linguine in pot of salted water with butter. Drain and set aside when al dente
2. Heat lobster stock until reduced in half.
3. Add heavy cream and reduce until slightly thickened. Whip lightly.
4. Add cooked linguini and drained seafood. Stir gently 10 minutes.
5. Serve immediately when seafood is done and sauce is creamy.

Salmon and Sweet Potatoes

Ingredients

- 2 Limes, 1 zested and juiced, one cut into wedges
- 3 Tbsp Mayonnaise
- 4 tsp Olive oil
- 1.25 lbs Salmon fillet, quartered
- 4 cups Broccoli florets
- 1 tsp Chili powder
- ½ cup Cilantro, chopped
- 1/4 cup Feta
- Salt to taste
- 2 Sweet potatoes, peeled and cubed

Procedure

1. Begin preheating your oven up to a temperature of 425° F. Then, prepare a sheet pan with grease. Mix mayonnaise and chili powder and set aside.

2. Season sweet potatoes and spread onto sheet pan to roast, drizzling olive oil onto them. Roast for 15 minutes.

3. Season broccoli and place onto sheet pan alongside salmon. Spread mayonnaise mixture on the salmon and bake until it easily flakes.

4. Add lime zest and juice to remaining mayonnaise and mix.

5. Serve salmon with cheese and cilantro on top, with a side of potatoes and broccoli.

6. Drizzle mayonnaise sauce on top and serve with lime wedges.

Roses of Norwegian Salmon

Serves 8 pax

Ingredients

- 16 ounces smoked Norwegian salmon slices

Procedure

1. Lay smoked salmon flat.
2. With a fillet knife, cut a 3-inch-long strip 1 inch wide.
3. Cut the strip from the edge of the fish, so the naturally uneven edge is part of the strip.
4. Roll the first inch of the strip tightly to form the center of a rose.
5. Roll the rest of the strip more loosely around the center.
6. Pinch together at the cut edge, leaving the thin, uneven edge to form the petals.
7. Hold the rose at the base.
8. With the tip of the fillet knife, gently peel back the rolled salmon just enough to open up the rose.
9. Repeat as necessary until all the salmon is used.

Pan Seared Salmon

Serves 6 pax

Ingredients

- 1/4 cup extra virgin olive oil
- Salt and freshly ground black pepper
- 6 x 6 oz center-cut salmon fillets
- 1/4 cup fresh lemon juice

Procedure

1. Darne is the middle cut of a large fish.
2. Place salmon darnes in a shallow bowl. Add lemon juice and olive oil. Season to taste with salt and pepper.
3. Toss until salmon is thoroughly coated. Let stand 15 minutes.
4. Place salmon skin side down in a skillet. Sear salmon 3 minutes on medium-high heat.
5. Shake pan and carefully loosen salmon with a spatula.
6. Lower heat to medium. Cover skillet and cook 4 minutes. Salmon darnes are done when skin is crisp and flesh medium rare.
7. Serve on bed of chunky fruit (recipe follows).

Chunky Fruit

Ingredients

- 3 tablespoons cilantro, chopped
- 1 large jalapeno pepper, seeded and minced
- 2 tablespoons fresh ginger, minced
- 6 tablespoons fresh squeezed orange juice
- 2 small limes fresh squeezed juice
- 2 teaspoons dried mint
- 1 large papaya, seeded and cubed
- 2 bananas, sliced
- 1 kiwi fruit, peeled and chopped
- 2 pints strawberries, quartered

Procedure

1. Mix orange juice, lime juice, zest, mint, cilantro, jalapeno and ginger together in a large bowl.
2. Add fruit. Toss well and refrigerate overnight.
3. To serve, divide fruit salad between 6 plates.
4. Top each fruit bed with the Salmon.

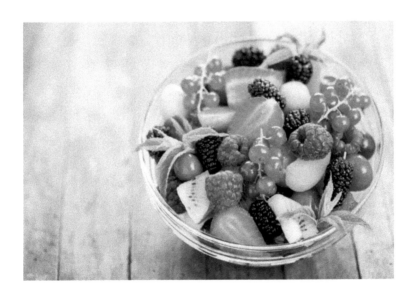

Lychee and Fennel Chutney

Ingredients

- 2 teaspoons turmeric powder
- 2 tablespoons mustard seeds
- 10 lychees
- 4 tablespoons fennel seeds
- 3 tablespoons fenugreek seeds
- 2 tablespoons red chili powder
- 2 cups mustard
- 1 cup evo oil
- Salt to taste

Procedure

1. Clean lychees and chop into 3/4" cubes. Rub with turmeric powder and salt. Let stand 30 minutes.
2. Drain excess moisture.
3. Grind fenugreek, fennel and mustard seeds to a coarse powder.
4. Heat mustard oil to smoking point. Remove from heat and let stand.
5. Mix ground seeds with red chili powder. Add half of the mustard oil to the powder mixture. Rub spice and oil mixture to lychee cubes until thoroughly mixed.
6. Place lychees in earthenware jar. Pour in other half of mustard oil. Add salt to taste and stir well. Cover jar with muslin cloth. Let stand 6 days in sunlight, stirring twice daily.
7. Continue to stir contents of jar twice daily for two weeks.
8. Serve as relish.

Steamed Potatoes

Ingredients

- 2 tablespoons fresh parsley, chopped
- 3 tablespoons extra-virgin olive oil
- 2 pounds new potatoes
- 2 tablespoons green onions, diced fine
- 1 garlic clove, minced
- Salt and freshly ground black pepper

Procedure

1. Pour an inch of water in steamer. Heat on medium-high heat.

2. Wash potatoes and place in the steamer basket. Sprinkle with a little sea salt.

3. When water simmers, place steamer basket on pot and cover. Cook 20 minutes. Potatoes are done when tender.

4. While steaming potatoes, heat olive oil and minced garlic in small skillet on low heat. Set aside when fragrant.

5. Remove potatoes from steaming basket. Place in large bowl. Add oil and garlic mixture, green onions and parsley.

6. Season to taste with salt and pepper. Toss potatoes until well coated.

7. Serve hot.

Roasted Salmon in Salsa Verde

Ingredients

- 1 tablespoon lime juice, plus lime wedges for serving
- 1 teaspoon ground coriander
- 1/4 cup minced fresh cilantro
- 1 (2 pound) skin on salmon fillet, 2 inches thick
- 1 jalapeño chile, stemmed, halved, and seeded
- 1 poblano chile, stemmed, seeded, and chopped
- 2 scallions, chopped
- 12 ounces tomatillos, husks and stems removed, washed well, dried, and quartered
- 3 tablespoons plus 2 teaspoons extra virgin olive oil
- 2 teaspoons chopped fresh oregano
- 2 garlic cloves, peeled
- Salt and pepper

Procedure

1. Adjust oven racks to lowest position and 6 inches from broiler element and heat broiler. Coat baking sheet with aluminium foil.

2. Toss tomatillos, poblano, jalapeño, 1 tablespoon oil, garlic, oregano, coriander, 1/4 teaspoon salt, and 1/4 teaspoon pepper together, then spread onto readied sheet.

3. Broil vegetables on upper rack until tomatillos and jalapeños are browned, ten to twelve minutes, stirring once in a while.

4. Move broiled vegetables to blender and allow to cool slightly. Put in 2 tablespoons cilantro, scallions, lime juice, and 1 tablespoon oil and blend until the desired smoothness is achieved, approximately one minute.

5. In the meantime, place clean rimmed baking sheet on lower oven rack and heat oven to 500 degrees.

6. Cut salmon crosswise into 4 fillets. Using sharp knife, make 4 or 5 shallow slashes, approximately an inch apart, through skin of each fillet, being cautious not to cut into flesh.

7. Pat salmon dry using paper towels, rub with remaining 2 teaspoons oil, and sprinkle with salt and pepper.

8. Reduce oven temperature to 275 degrees and remove preheated baking sheet. Cautiously place salmon, skin side down, on baking sheet.

9. Roast on lower rack until center is still translucent when checked with tip of paring knife and records 125 degrees (for medium rare), 9 to 13 minutes.

10. Move salmon to plates, spoon some of sauce over top and drizzle with remaining 2 tablespoons minced cilantro.

11. Serve with rest of the sauce and lime wedges.

Salmon Terrine and Salmon Caviar Sauce

Serves 6 pax

Ingredients

- 1 tablespoon lemon zest
- 2 tablespoons lemon juice
- 1/3 cup fresh dill, finely chopped
- 1 pound sliced smoked Norwegian salmon
- 2 cups cream cheese
- 1/4 cup cream
- 2 tablespoons capers
- Freshly ground black pepper

Procedure

1. Place cream cheese, cream, lemon zest, lemon juice, dill and capers in a food processor. Season to taste with pepper and combine. Butter a 6 cups terrine pan.

2. Line base and sides with plastic wrap overhanging two inches at ends. Layer enough smoked salmon to cover bottom of pan. Layer 1/3 cup cream cheese mixture equally over salmon.

3. Repeat layering process until all the salmon is used. The top layer should be salmon.

4. Fold plastic wrap over salmon, pressing down gently. Refrigerate overnight.

5. Before serving, turn onto a platter and remove wrap. Trim ends and cut into slices.

6. Drizzle with red salmon caviar sauce (recipe follows).

7. Serve.

Red Salmon Caviar Sauce

Serves 6 pax

Ingredients

- ½ cup mayonnaise
- 4 tablespoons fresh dill, chopped
- 1 pinch white pepper
- 1 cup sour cream
- 8 ounces crème fraiche
- 3 ounces red salmon caviar

Procedure

1. Combine sour cream, creme fraiche, mayonnaise, dill, and white pepper in a bowl. Stir well.
2. Carefully mix in caviar.
3. Cover and refrigerate 1 hour.
4. Drizzle over salmon terrine (recipe above).

Seafood Stuffed Salmon

Serves 12 pax

Ingredients

- 2 cups cooked long grain rice
- 1 package (8 ounces) imitation crabmeat
- 3 tablespoons cream cheese, softened
- 5 tablespoons butter, melted
- 12 salmon fillets (8 ounces each and 1-1/2 inches thick)
- 4 tablespoons olive oil
- 2 teaspoons dill weed
- 2 teaspoons salt
- 2 garlic cloves, minced
- 1/2teaspoon each dried basil, marjoram, oregano, thyme and rosemary, crushed
- 1/2teaspoon celery seed, crushed

Procedure

1. Preheat an oven to 400°F.

2. Mix celery seed, rosemary, thyme, oregano, marjoram, basil, garlic, butter, cream cheese, crab and rice in a big bowl.

3. Horizontally cut a pocket, within 1/2-in. from opposite side, in each fillet. Use stuffing mixture to fill; use toothpicks to secure.

4. Put salmon on 2 (15 x 10 x 1 -in) greased baking pans; brush oil. Sprinkle salt and dill.

5. Bake till fish just starts to easily flake with a fork for 18-22 minutes.

6. Before serving, discard toothpicks.

Salmon and Strawberry Basil Relish

Serves 6 pax

Ingredients

- 1/4 teaspoon salt
- 6 x 4 ounces salmon fillets
- 1 tablespoon butter, melted
- 1/8 teaspoon freshly ground pepper

For the Relish:

- 1 tablespoon honey
- 1 cup finely chopped fresh strawberries
- 1 tablespoon minced fresh basil
- Dash freshly ground pepper

Procedure

1. Brush melted butter on fillets; sprinkle with pepper and salt.
2. On medium-high heat, heat a big skillet. Add fillets in batches if needed, skin side up; cook till fish just starts to easily flake with a fork or for 2-3 minutes per side.
3. Toss pepper, honey, basil and strawberries in a small bowl.
4. Serve salmon with relish.

Layered Salmon and Cobb Salad

Ingredients

- 2 teaspoons chopped fresh dill
- Salt and ground black pepper to taste
- 3 cups fresh green beans, trimmed
- 3/4 cup buttermilk
- 1/4 cup mayonnaise
- 5 hard-boiled eggs, halved
- 6 slices cooked bacon, cut into thin strips
- 3 spring onions, thinly sliced
- 2 tablespoons white wine vinegar
- ½ clove garlic, crushed
- 6x 5 pounds salmon fillets
- ½ teaspoon vegetable oil
- 4 cups chopped green leaf lettuce
- 1 pound tomatoes, cut into bite-sized pieces
- 1 (15 ounce) can corn, drained
- 2 cucumbers, halved and sliced

Procedure

1. In a jar, mix garlic, buttermilk, white wine vinegar, and mayonnaise. Seal the jar and then shake thoroughly. Mix in pepper, dill, and salt. Chill the dressing.

2. Put a steamer insert in a saucepan and add water until just below bottom of the steamer. Heat the water to boil. Place in green beans, cover the pan and then steam for about 4 to 5 minutes until tender. Drain off water and cool.

3. Preheat the grill over medium heat and coat the grate lightly with oil. Baste the salmon with the vegetable oil. Add pepper and salt to taste.

4. Cook the salmon on the grill for about 6 to 8 minutes on each side until the flesh easily flakes with a fork.

5. In a large glass trifle bowl, spread lettuce, green beans, tomatoes, corn, hard-boiled eggs and cucumbers.

6. Top with the salmon. Stud with spring onions and bacon.

7. Serve along with the dressing.

Apricot Glazed Salmon and Herb Rice

Serves 6 pax

Ingredients

- 1/3 cup apricot spreadable fruit
- ½ teaspoon grated fresh gingerroot
- 2 cups reduced-sodium chicken broth
- 1 teaspoon minced fresh thyme
- 3 tablespoons sliced almonds, toasted
- 1 cup uncooked long grain rice
- 6 x 4 ounces salmon fillets
- 1/4 teaspoon salt
- 1/8 teaspoon pepper
- 1/3 cup white wine
- 2 teaspoons butter
- 2 tablespoons chopped dried apricots
- 2 tablespoons minced fresh parsley
- 1 tablespoon minced chives

Procedure

1. Coat a 13 x 9-inch pan with cooking spray and lay salmon inside.
2. Season with pepper and salt to taste. Meanwhile, mix together spreadable fruit, ginger and wine in a small bowl. Pour mixture over the salmon.
3. Bake for 15 to 20 minutes at 375° until fish separates easily with fork.
4. While the fish is baking, combine rice, butter and broth in a small pot and bring to a boil. Turn the heat down and let it simmer, covered, 10 minutes.
5. Add the apricots and continue cooking until rice is tender and all the liquid gets absorbed, 5 to 8 minutes.
6. Mix in chives, thyme and parsley.
7. Serve rice with salmon and garnish with almonds.

Salmon and Asparagus Pasta

Ingredients

- 2 cups uncooked bow tie pasta
- 2 pounds fresh asparagus, trimmed and cut into 2-inch pieces
- 2 medium leeks (white portion only), thinly sliced
- 2 teaspoons olive oil
- 2 teaspoons cornstarch
- ½ cup water
- 4 x 1 pound salmon fillet
- ½ teaspoon salt, divided
- ½ teaspoon pepper, divided
- ½ cup chicken broth
- 2 tablespoons snipped fresh dill
- 1 tablespoon lemon juice

Procedure

1. Season the salmon with a quarter teaspoon (1/4 teaspoon) of salt and pepper. Lightly coat the grill rack using an oiled paper towel and tongs with a long handle.

2. Start grilling the salmon while covered on a medium heat or broil for about 4-6 inches from the heat for 12- 18 minutes with a fork.

3. Prepare the pasta as specified on its package. Sauté the leeks and asparagus in a large, oiled skillet until the asparagus get its tender-crisp texture. Season with the remaining salt and pepper.

4. Combine the lemon juice, broth, water, cornstarch, and dill, in a small bowl. Stir well until the mixture smoothens.

5. Add the sautéed asparagus and leeks. Boil and simmer; continuously stir until it bubbles and thickens.

6. Turn the heat to a minimum and cook for another 2 minutes longer while stirring. Drain the pasta and toss with asparagus mixture.

7. Serve with salmon.

Lemony Salmon and Basil

Serves 4 pax

Ingredients

- 1/2teaspoon salt
- 1/4 teaspoon pepper
- 3 tablespoons thinly sliced fresh basil
- 2 medium lemons, thinly sliced
- 4 x 6 ounces salmon fillets
- 2 teaspoons olive oil
- 1 tablespoon grated lemon peel
- Additional fresh basil

Procedure

1. Preheat an oven to 375°. Put salmon into an oiled 15 x 10 x 1 -in. Baking pan.
2. Drizzle with oil; sprinkle 2 tbsp. of basil, pepper, salt and lemon peel. Put lemon slices over the top.
3. Bake till fish starts to flake easily with a fork for 15-20 minutes; put extra basil over the top if desired.

Salmon and Balsamic Orange Sauce

Ingredients

- 4 teaspoons honey
- 8 x 6 ounces salmon fillets, skin removed
- 4 teaspoons grated orange zest
- 4 teaspoons balsamic vinegar
- 1 teaspoon salt

For the Sauce:

- 2 teaspoons honey
- 1 teaspoon balsamic vinegar
- 1 teaspoon cornstarch
- 1 cup orange juice
- 1/4 teaspoon salt

Procedure

1. Preheat an oven to 425°. Put ham into a 15x10x1-in. greased baking pan.
2. Mix salt, honey, vinegar and orange zest in a small bowl; spread over fillets.
3. Roast till fish just starts to easily flake with a fork for 15-18 minutes.
4. Meanwhile, combine orange juice and cornstarch in a small saucepan; boil; cook while stirring till thickened for one minute.
5. Mix in salt, vinegar and honey; serve with salmon.

Poached Salmon

Ingredients

- 1 lemon slice
- 1 sprig dill
- ½ teaspoon salt
- 1 cup water
- ½ cup dry white wine
- 1 yellow onion slice
- 4 x 6 ounces salmon fillets

Procedure

1. Mix together the wine and water in the slow cooker. Set on high to heat for 20 to 30 minutes.
2. Add the salmon, salt, dill, lemon and onion.
3. Set the cooker on high. Cover and let it cook for about 20 minutes, until the salmon becomes opaque and cooked completely according to taste.
4. Serve it hot and can also be served cold.

Elegant Smoked Salmon Strata

Ingredients

- 2 cups shredded Gruyere or Swiss cheese
- 2 cups shredded white cheddar cheese
- 10 green onions, sliced
- 4 cups cubed ciabatta bread
- 2 tablespoons butter, melted
- 2 tablespoons olive oil
- ½ pound smoked salmon or lox, coarsely chopped
- 8 large eggs
- 1/4 teaspoon pepper
- Creme fraiche or sour cream and minced chives
- 4 cups 2% milk
- 4 teaspoons Dijon mustard
- 1/4 teaspoon salt

Procedure

1. Toss bread cubes with oil and butter in a big bowl; move to a greased 13 x 9-inch baking dish.

2. Add salmon, onions and cheeses on top. In a separate bowl, whisk together pepper, salt, mustard, milk and eggs; add over top.

3. Keep in refrigerator, covered, overnight.

4. Remove from the fridge 30 minutes prior to baking. Cover the dish and bake for 30 minutes at 350°.

5. Remove cover and bake for another 25 to 30 minutes until an inserted knife in the middle exits clean.

6. Allow to stand for 10 minutes prior to serving.

7. Serve with chives and creme fraiche.

Salmon Omelets and Creme Fraiche

Ingredients

- 2 tablespoons butter
- 6 x 1 pound salmon fillets, cooked and flaked
- 2 cups shredded Swiss cheese
- 12 large eggs
- 2 tablespoons whole milk
- Salt and pepper to taste
- 2 tablespoons snipped fresh dill
- 3/4 cup creme fraiche or sour cream
- 6 fresh dill sprigs

Procedure

1. Beat pepper, salt, milk, and eggs in a large bowl until combined.
2. For each omelet: Let a teaspoon of butter melt on medium heat in an 8-inch ovenproof skillet.
3. Add ½ cup of the egg mixture into the pan. Dust with a teaspoon of snipped dill, 1/2cup of cheese, and 1/3 cup of salmon.
4. Lift the edges to allow the uncooked portion to flow underneath them while the eggs set. Cook until the eggs are almost set.
5. Broil 6 inches from the heat source until the eggs are set completely, or for 1-2 minutes.
6. Fold the omelet in half and place onto a plate. Add a dill sprig and 2 tablespoons of creme fraiche on top.
7. Repeat the process for the remaining omelets.

Smoked Mushroom Salmon Tarts

Ingredients

- 4 cups sliced fresh mushrooms
- 2/3 cup smoked salmon or lox
- 1/3 cup crumbled feta cheese
- 8 large eggs, divided use
- 1 x 14.1 ounces package refrigerated pie pastry
- 1 tablespoon olive oil
- 1 medium red onion, thinly sliced
- 1 tablespoon butter
- 4 teaspoons drained capers, divided
- ½ teaspoon salt, divided
- ½ teaspoon pepper, divided
- 2 teaspoons snipped fresh dill, divided

Procedure

1. In 2 x 9 inches fluted tart pans that comes with removable bottoms, unroll pastry sheets; trim off all edges.

2. Keep in refrigerator for 30 minutes and set the oven to 400° and start preheating.

3. Line two layers of foil on an unpricked pastry. Fill with uncooked rice, dried beans or pie weights.

4. Arrange on a lower oven rack and bake for 10 to 15 minutes or until the color of edges turn to golden brown.

5. Remove weights and foil and bake for another 2 to 4 minutes or until the color of the bottom turn to golden brown.

6. Arrange on a wire rack to cool. Lower the oven heat to 375°.

7. Heat oil in a big skillet over medium high heat. Add onion and cook for 5 to 7 minutes or until light brown in color and softened, remember to stir while cooking.

8. Remove from pan. Add mushrooms and butter and cook for 6 to 8 minutes or until mushrooms are softened, remember to stir while cooking. Cool slightly.

9. Place each tart pan on a separate baking sheets. Distribute mushrooms and onion evenly between crusts; add cheese and salmon on top.

10. In a bowl, whisk together 1/4 teaspoon of each pepper and salt (optional), 2 teaspoons of capers and 4 eggs, stir in 1 teaspoon of dill.

11. Pour mixture over one of the tarts, repeat the same process for remaining ingredients, pour over the second tart.

12. Bake for 15 to 20 minutes or until a knife is still clean after being inserted into the center.

13. Allow to stand for 5 minutes prior to cutting.

Eggplant Eggs Benedict

Serves 8 pax

Ingredients

- 8 x 1 inch thick slices eggplant
- 1 teaspoon white vinegar
- 8 large eggs
- 2 tablespoons olive oil
- 1/4 teaspoon salt
- 1/4 teaspoon white pepper
- 4 English muffins, split and toasted
- 8 ounces smoked salmon fillet, flaked
- ½ cup sour cream

For the Hollandaise Sauce:
- 3/4 cup butter, melted
- 1 teaspoon salt
- 1 large egg yolks
- 1/4 cup water
- 2 tablespoons lemon juice
- 1/4 teaspoon white pepper
- 2 tablespoons minced chives

Procedure

1. In a small bowl, mix pepper, salt and oil; brush over both sides of eggplant. Transfer to an ungreased 15x10x1-in. baking pan.

2. Broil 4-6 in. from the heat for 5-7 minutes on each side or until it is lightly browned and tender.

3. In the meantime, in a large skillet with high sides, pour 2-3 in. of water; add vinegar. Bring to a boil; lower the heat and gently simmer.

4. Break cold egg, one at a time, into a saucer or custard cup; keeping the cup near to the water's surface, slip each egg into water.

5. Cook without a cover until whites set completely and yolks start to get thick (but are not hard), about 4 minutes. Using a slotted spoon, remove each egg from the water.

6. Put 1 tablespoon sour cream, 3 tablespoons salmon, egg and an eggplant slice over each muffin half. Put aside and keep them warm.

7. Beat lemon juice, water and egg yolks constantly in a double boiler over simmering water until the mixture begins to thicken and covers the back of a metal spoon. Lower the heat to low. Drizzle slowly in melted butter, whipping constantly. Beat in salt and pepper.

8. Scoop 3 tablespoons sauce onto 8 serving plates. Put the prepared muffin and top with chives.

Salmon Stew

Ingredients

- 3 cups salmon broth
- 28 oz Crushed tomatoes
- 1 tsp Dried basil
- 1 tsp Dried oregano
- 2 cloves Garlic
- 0.5 tsp Black pepper
- 0.5 tsp Salt
- 8 oz Medium
- 6 oz salmon filets
- 2 stalks Celery
- 1 Red bell pepper
- 1 Onion
- 1 Tbsp Olive oil

Procedure

1. Dice/mince the garlic, celery, onions, and peppers.
2. Prepare an over-sized pot or dutch oven using the medium temperature setting to warm the oil.
3. Sauté the garlic, bell pepper, onion, celery, basil, and oregano until the onion is softened and translucent.
4. Stir in the crushed tomatoes and broth, bring to a simmer, and simmer until vegetables are soft, about 10 minutes.
5. Stir in the salmon and simmer until is cooked, about 5 minutes.

Spicy Salmon Dip

Ingredients

- ½ teaspoon salt
- 1 tablespoon minced chives
- 5 tablespoons butter
- ½ serrano chili, seeded and minced
- ½ teaspoon grated lemon zest
- 8 ounces salmon, cleaned and chopped
- Salt and freshly ground black pepper

Procedure

1. In a moderate-sized-sized sauté pan, melt the butter on moderate heat.
2. Mix in the chives, salt, chili pepper, and lemon zest; sauté for a couple of minutes.
3. Lower the heat to low and put in the salmon; sauté for about three minutes or until opaque.
4. Move the mixture to a food processor and crudely purée. Sprinkle with salt and pepper.
5. Firmly pack the purée into a small container. Cover using plastic wrap, and place in your fridge for 4 hours or overnight.
6. To serve, remove the salmon dip from the fridge and let it sit for five to ten minutes.
7. Serve the dip with an assortment of crackers and toast points or some favorite veggies.

Roasted Salmon

Serves 4 pax

Ingredients

- ½ teaspoon sugar
- 1 tablespoon extra-virgin olive oil
- 12 ounces skinless salmon fillets, 1 inch thick
- 4 Lemon wedges
- Salt and pepper

Procedure

1   Place the oven rack in the center of the oven and pre-heat your oven to 425 degrees.
2   Pat salmon dry using paper towels, sprinkle with salt and pepper, and drizzle sugar uniformly 1 side of each fillet.
3   Heat oil in 12-inch oven-safe frying pan on moderate to high heat until just smoking.
4   Place salmon sugared side down in frying pan and press lightly to ensure even contact with skillet.
5   Cook until browned on first side, approximately two minutes.
6   Gently flip salmon using 2 spatulas, move frying pan to oven, and roast until fish flakes apart when softly poked using paring knife and registers 140 degrees, 7 to 10 minutes.
7   Serve with lemon wedges.

Salmon Patè

Ingredients

- 1 teaspoon sugar
- 2 cups minced salmon
- 2 tablespoons vegetable oil
- 1/4 teaspoon white pepper
- ½ teaspoon salt
- 1 red chili, seeded and thoroughly minced
- 8 pieces sugarcane

Procedure

1. Preheat your oven to 375 degrees.
2. Put the salmon, salt, sugar, white pepper, and chili in a food processor; process until the desired smoothness is achieved.
3. Sprinkle in one to 2 tablespoons of the vegetable oil. Process the salmon mixture until it reaches the consistency necessary to make a meatball, using nearly oil.
4. Split the salmon mixture into 4 equivalent portions.
5. Use your hands to mold a "salmon ball" around the center of each of the sugarcane pieces.
6. Put the "skewers" on a baking sheet and roast for roughly twenty minutes.
7. If you prefer them a little extra browned, broil them (after they are done baking) until the desired color is reached.
8. To serve, spoon some of the sweet-and-sour sauce into the middle of 4 plates.
9. Put the sugarcane "skewer" on top of the sauce.

Roasted Squash and Wild Salmon Risotto

Ingredients

- 4 roasted salmon fillets
- Salt and freshly ground black pepper
- 1 onion, peeled and chopped
- $1/3$ mug of grated Parmesan cheese
- A couple handfuls of rocket leaves, chopped
- 1 mug of risotto rice
- 2 mugs of butternut squash, peeled and diced into $1/2$ inches cubes
- 1 mug Olive oil
- $1/2$ mug of white wine
- 2 mugs of simmering chicken or vegetable stock
- 2 tbsp double cream

Procedure

1 Toss the diced squash in a little olive oil, season well with salt and pepper and place on a baking tray. Pop into a 375°F gas 5 oven for 20 minutes or so, turning occasionally. Remove from the oven just when the outer edges start to brown off.

2 Set aside to cool down and keep your picking fingers away from them, otherwise you won't have any to put into the risotto.

3 While they are cooling, sauté the onion with a glug of olive oil in a large heavy-based pot over a medium heat for 3–5 minutes.

4 Add the rice and wine and slowly simmer until the wine has almost evaporated, stirring constantly.

5 Now you start adding the stock to the rice a little at a time – as with the wine, you need to stir constantly and only add stock when the rice starts to thicken and get sticky. Keep the stock simmering in a separate saucepan.

6 Continue doing this until the rice is cooked through and your arm is about to fall off.

7 Finally, when the rice is cooked through, add the cream and half the Parmesan, stir through the rocket and baked squash, season and remove from the heat when the risotto is nice and sticky.

8 Sprinkle the remaining Parmesan and roasted salmon over each dish and serve.

Salmon in Mustard Sauce

Serves 4 pax

Ingredients

- ½ cup Fish Stock or Vegetable Stock
- 3/4 teaspoon kosher salt
- 2 tablespoons Dijon mustard
- 2 tablespoons vegetable oil
- 2 tablespoons unsalted butter
- 1/4 cup heavy cream
- ½ cup dry white wine
- All-purpose flour, for dredging
- 4 x 6-ounce skinless salmon fillets
- Freshly ground black pepper to taste

Procedure

1. Flavor the salmon fillets on both sides with 1/2teaspoon of the salt and some pepper. Heat a big nonstick frying pan on moderate to high heat.
2. Put in the vegetable oil. While the oil heats, spread the flour on a plate and gently dredge the salmon in it, patting off the surplus. Lightly put in the fillets to the frying pan.
3. Cook, flipping over once, until they are browned on both sides but not thoroughly cooked, approximately two minutes per side. Remove them to a plate.
4. Pour the surplus oil from the frying pan and wipe it clean using a paper towel. Melt the butter in the frying pan on moderate heat.
5. Put in the wine and bring to a simmer. Put in the fish stock and cream, and flavor with the rest of the 1/4 teaspoon salt.
6. Simmer, whisking once in a while, until the sauce is a little thickened, approximately 4 minutes.

7. Whisk in the mustard. Put in the salmon, flesh side up, and simmer, once in a while spooning the sauce over the salmon, until the fish is just thoroughly cooked—about three minutes, depending on the thickness of the salmon.
8. Serve instantly.

Stuffed Salmon

Ingredients

- 1 red bell pepper, stemmed, seeded, and chopped fine
- 1 red onion, chopped fine
- 1 tablespoon minced fresh parsley
- 1/3 cup pitted brine-cured green olives, chopped
- 10 ounces whole salmon, gutted
- 4 Lemon wedges
- Salt and pepper
- ½ preserved lemon, pulp and white pith removed, rind rinsed and minced
- 3 tablespoons extra-virgin olive oil

Procedure

1   Place the oven rack in the center of the oven and pre-heat your oven to 500 degrees.

2   Heat 2 tablespoons oil in 12-inch frying pan on moderate to high heat until it starts to shimmer.

3   Put in bell pepper and onion and cook until vegetables are softened and well browned, eight to ten minutes.

4   Mix in preserved lemon and cook until aromatic, approximately half a minute.

5   Remove from the heat, mix in olives and parsley and sprinkle with salt and pepper to taste.

6   Grease rimmed baking sheet with remaining 1 tablespoon oil. Wash each mackerel under cold running water and pat dry using paper towels inside and out.

7   Open cavity of each salmon, season flesh with salt and pepper, and spoon 1/4 of filling into opening.

8   Place salmon on readied sheet, spaced at least 2 inches apart. Bake until thickest part of salmon registers 130 to 135 degrees, 10 to 12 minutes.

9   Cautiously move salmon to serving platter and allow to rest for about five minutes.

10 Serve with lemon wedges.

Thank you, dear fish lover.

I am glad you accepted my teachings.

These meals have been personally codified in my worldwide trips.

I wanted to share them with you, to let people know more about meat and how to treat it properly.

Now you had come to know about Salmon in all of its shapes, let me give you one more tip.

This manual takes part of an unmissable cookbooks collection.

These fish-based recipes, mixed to all the tastes I met around the world, will give you a complete idea of the possibilities this world offers to us.

You have now the opportunity to add hundreds new elements to your cooking skills knowledge.

Check out the other books!

Ernest Pescara

Lightning Source UK Ltd.
Milton Keynes UK
UKHW021841100621
385314UK00002B/450